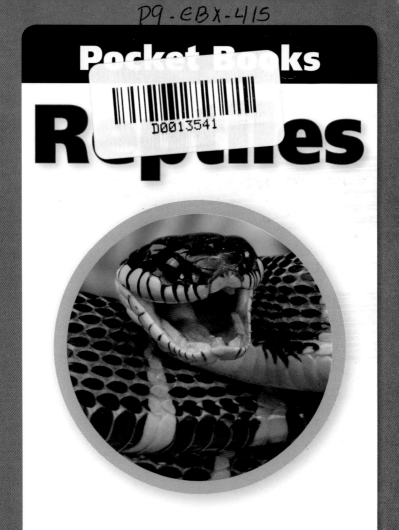

Pocket Books

Reptiles

Kane Miller
A DIVISION OF EDC PUBLISHING

P9-EBX-415

D0013541

First American Edition 2015
Kane Miller, A Division of EDC Publishing

Copyright © Green Android Ltd 2014

For information contact:
Kane Miller, A Division of EDC Publishing
P.O. Box 470663
Tulsa, OK 74147-0663
www.kanemiller.com
www.edcpub.com
www.usbornebooksandmore.com

Please note that every effort has been made to check the accuracy of the information contained in this book, and to credit the copyright holders correctly. Green Android Ltd apologize for any unintentional errors or omissions, and would be happy to include revisions to content and/or acknowledgements in subsequent editions of this book.

Printed and bound in China, October 2014
Library of Congress Control Number: 2014939761
ISBN: 978-1-61067-350-1

Images © Fotolia.com: Boomslang © Duncan Noakes; Chinese Soft-shelled Turtle © think4photop; Common Musk Turtle © hirron; Desert Tortoise © schmaelterphoto; Galapagos Tortoise © dlrz4114; Gharial © Rich Lindie; Green Green Vine Snake © thawats; Hawksbill Turtle © serg_dibrova; Komodo Dragon © vrabelpeter1; Leopard Tortoise © gallas; Loggerhead Sea Turtle © hotshotsworldwide; Mojave Rattlesnake, Prairie Rattlesnake © Rusty Dodson; Olive Ridley Sea Turtle © Ivalin; Amazon Tree Boa © fivespots; Texas Tortoise © Vibe Images; Timber Rattlesnake © Heiko Kiera.

Images © Shutterstock.com: Dwarf Crocodile © Alan Jeffery; Black Mamba © Andre Coetzer; Common Garter Snake © Aneese; Boa Constrictor © Anton_Ivanov; Mangrove Snake © Antti Pulkkinen; Indian Star Tortoise © ARTEKI; Tuatara © Cameramannz; Panther Chameleon, Tokay Gecko © Cathy Keifer; Eastern Blue-tongued Skink © Chris Humphries; Black Caiman © defpicture; Eastern Green Mamba © Dennis Donohue; Web-footed Gecko © dirk; African Helmeted Turtle © EcoPrint; Common Kingsnake, Egyptian Cobra, Gaboon Viper © Eric Isselee; Red Corn Snake © erllre74; Northern Water Snake © Evoken; Stump-tailed Skink © dr322; Saltwater Crocodile © GTS Production; Turkish Gecko © Ilias Strachinis; Lace Monitor © Stephen Denness; Rhinoceros Viper © Ivan Kuzmin; White-throated Monitor © ivespots; Gopher Tortoise © J. Norman Reid; Thorny Devil © Janelle Lugge; Glossy Snake, Common Chuckwalla © Jason Mintzer; Wood Turtle, Smooth Green Snake, Queen Snake © Jason Patrick Ross; Diamondback Terrapin, Coachwhip © Jay Ondreicka; Frilled Lizard © kkaplin; Nile Monitor © KobchaiMa; Royal Python © Kuznetsov Alexey; Common Leopard Gecko © Reinhold Leitner; Burmese Python © rina oxilixo Danilova; Viviparous Lizard © MarkMirror; Eastern Racer, Milk Snake, Yellow Rat Snake, Wandering Garter Snake, Plains Garter Snake, Southern Copperhead, Madrean Alligator Lizard, Jackson's Chameleon, Texas Horned Lizard, Five-lined Skink © Matt Jeppson; Common European Adder © Matteo photos; Veiled Chameleon © MattiaATH; Green Anole © Leena Robinson; Butler's Garter Snake © Michiel de Wit; Eastern Diamondback © Mike V. Shuman; Slow Worm © Milos Batinic; Broad-headed Skink © Momo5287; Iberian Worm Lizard © neil hardwick; Asian Water Dragon © nutsiam; Emerald Tree Boa © outdoorsman; Spectacled Caiman © Pablo Hidalgo; Green Anaconda, Eastern Indigo Snake, Blunthead Tree Snake, Pine Woods Snake, Eastern Coral Snake © Patrick K. Campbell; Carpet Python © Peter Zachar; Water Monitor © Petr Malyshev; United Snake © Psychotic Nature; American Alligator © Raffaella Calzoni; Eyelash Viper, Armadillo Girdled Lizard, Carpet Chameleon © reptiles4all; Chinese Crocodile Lizard © rickyd; Marine Iguana © Roland Spiegler; Gila monster, Eastern Ribbon Snake, Chinese Alligator © Rusty Dodson; Northern Map Turtle, Eastern Fox Snake, Massasauga Rattlesnake, Tiger Rattlesnake, Parson's Chameleon, Giant Ameiva, Nile Crocodile © Ryan M. Bolton; Six-lined Racerunner © Sari ONeal; King Cobra © Skynavin; Crested Gecko © Somer McCain; Rough Greensnake, Common Collared Lizard © Steve Bower; Puff Adder © Stu Porter; Western Diamondback © Tom Reichner; Common Green Iguana © tratong; African Bush Viper © Willie Davis; Hermann's Tortoise © xpixel; ; Common Snapping Turtle © camera obscura USA; Leatherback Sea Turtle © IrinaK; Sea Turtle © Kristina Vackova; Rosy Boa © Ryan M. Bolton; Reticulated Python © fivespots; Bekay's Brown Snake © Ryan M. Bolton.

Introducing reptiles

Reptiles have lived on Earth for at least 300 million years. Over time their bodies have adapted for survival in their environments. There are over 8,000 species of reptiles found on Earth. Many reptile species spend most of their time on land, but some spend a great deal of time in the water. Reptiles can be found in most types of habitat except for polar ice and tundra.

Marine iguanas live on land and in the water.

A Texas horned lizard warms its body in the bright sunlight.

Gharials have skin covered with smooth scales that do not overlap.

Characteristics of reptiles

Reptiles are vertebrates. This means that they have a backbone or spine.

Reptiles are cold-blooded and so are unable to automatically control their temperature in the way that humans do. Reptiles depend on heat from sunlight to become warm and active. If they get too hot, they find shade or a burrow to help them cool down.

The skin of a reptile is covered with scales. The scales act as armor to protect the animal from injury. All reptiles have lungs that are used for breathing air.

How to use this book

The pages of this book include concise information and key features on reptiles from around the world.

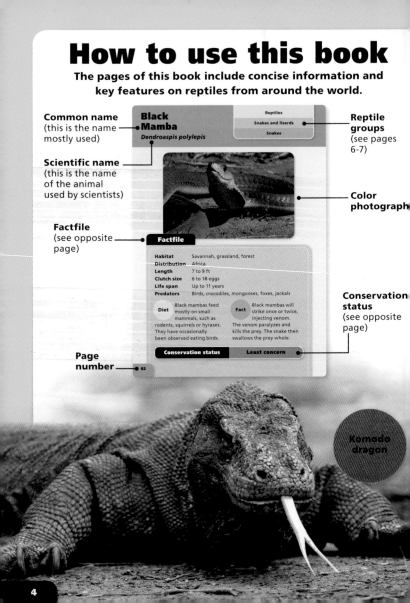

Common name
(this is the name mostly used)

Scientific name
(this is the name of the animal used by scientists)

Factfile
(see opposite page)

Page number

Black Mamba
Dendroaspis polylepis

Reptiles
Snakes and lizards
Snakes

Reptile groups
(see pages 6-7)

Color photograph

Factfile

Habitat	Savannah, grassland, forest
Distribution	Africa
Length	7 to 9 ft
Clutch size	6 to 18 eggs
Life span	Up to 11 years
Predators	Birds, crocodiles, mongooses, foxes, jackals

Diet Black mambas feed mostly on small mammals, such as rodents, squirrels or hyraxes. They have occasionally been observed eating birds.

Fact Black mambas will strike once or twice, injecting venom. The venom paralyzes and kills the prey. The snake then swallows the prey whole.

Conservation status   Least concern

Conservation status
(see opposite page)

Komodo dragon

4

Factfile

Each page comes with a detailed factfile containing descriptions, information, facts and figures.

Habitat
This indicates the environment that the reptile lives in. Some reptiles will live in many different habitats.

Distribution
This describes where in the world the reptile is found in its natural habitat.

Length
A measurement of the reptile's body.

Diet
A description of the food that the reptile eats and where it gets the food.

Clutch size or Litter size
The clutch size is the number of eggs that a reptile lays, while the litter size is the number of live young a reptile gives birth to.

Life span
This is the average natural length of the reptile's life.

Predators
This category lists the names of other animals that prey on this reptile. When the name of the predator is followed by "(young only)" it indicates that the predator only preys on the reptile when it is young.

Fact
Every factfile comes with an interesting fact about each reptile.

Conservation status

Each animal in this book has been given a conservation status. This status indicates the threat of extinction to the species in its native home.

Not evaluated
The animals within this category have not yet been evaluated for their conservation status.

Least concern
This is the lowest risk category. Animals in this category are widespread and abundant.

Near threatened
The animals in this category are likely to become endangered in the near future.

Vulnerable
There is a high risk that animals within this category will become endangered in the wild.

Endangered
There is a high risk that animals within this category will become extinct in the wild.

There is an extremely high risk of animals in this category becoming extinct in the wild.

Reptile groups

There are four main groups of reptile: turtles and tortoises, tuatara, snakes and lizards, and crocodilians.

Turtles and tortoises
250 species

All turtles and tortoises have a hard shell that acts as protection. Most are able to pull their head, legs and tail back inside the shell, making it nearly impossible for a predator to get at them. Most tortoises live on land, while turtles live at sea. A tortoise has strong legs to support its weight, while turtles have flippers to help them move through the water.

The Galápagos tortoise is the largest living tortoise.

Tuatara
2 species

Tuataras are the only surviving members of a group of reptiles that lived over 200 million years ago. Tuatara are found only on certain small islands off the coast of New Zealand.

Snakes and lizards
Around 8,900 species

Lizards typically have four legs, eyelids that can move and a long tail. Many lizards have evolved into amazing climbers, with pads on their feet that cling to smooth surfaces. Snakes are highly evolved predators. They may have evolved from lizards that burrowed underground. Their streamlined bodies would have helped them to move through the soil.

A tokay gecko climbing a branch.

Crocodilians
24 species

Crocodiles, alligators, caimans and gharials all belong to the group called crocodilians. These large reptiles are fearsome hunters who are able to catch animals as large as antelopes. They are ambush hunters, which means they lie in wait for prey to pass by and then they attack. Large prey is dragged under the water until it drowns.

Spectacled caimans have around 75 sharp teeth.

The Nile crocodile hides in water, waiting for prey.

Contents

Green
Sea Turtle
Chelonia mydas

Reptiles

Turtles and tortoises

Turtles

Factfile

Habitat	Tropical water
Distribution	Indian, Atlantic, Pacific Oceans
Length	Up to 5 ft (carapace length)
Clutch size	100 to 200 eggs
Life span	Up to 75 years
Predators	Sharks, orcas

Diet
Green turtles are mostly herbivorous. They spend most of their time feeding on algae in the sea and the grasses that grow in shallow waters.

Fact
Every 3 to 6 years the female green turtle comes ashore to dig a nest in the sand and lay eggs. She lays up to 200 eggs each time she nests.

Conservation status   **Endangered**

Hawksbill Turtle

Eretmochelys imbricata

Factfile

Habitat	Reefs, shoals, lagoons
Distribution	Indian, Atlantic, Pacific Oceans
Length	Up to 45 in (carapace length)
Clutch size	Up to 140 eggs
Life span	30 to 50 years
Predators	Sharks, crocodiles, large fish, octopuses

Diet Although the hawksbill sea turtle does occasionally eat some fish, mollusks, sea plants and crustaceans, it feeds primarily on sponges.

Fact Young hawksbill turtles cannot dive deep into the water. They spend their early years floating amongst sea plants near the water's surface.

Conservation status

9

Loggerhead Sea Turtle

Caretta caretta

Reptiles

Turtles and tortoises

Turtles

Factfile

Habitat	Open ocean, coast, reefs
Distribution	Indian, Atlantic, Pacific Oceans
Length	28 to 37 in (carapace length)
Clutch size	Up to 120 eggs
Life span	30 to 62 years
Predators	Bears, foxes, raccoons, dogs

Diet Loggerhead sea turtles eat crabs, barnacles, whelks and many other invertebrates, such as sponges, jellyfish, shrimp, insects, fish and fish eggs.

Fact Long-distance migration makes loggerhead turtles vulnerable to being captured in fishing nets. This can lead to injuries or death by drowning.

Conservation status   **Endangered**

Olive Ridley Sea Turtle

Lepidochelys olivacea

Factfile

Habitat	Coast
Distribution	Indian, Atlantic, Pacific Oceans
Length	Up to 30 in (carapace length)
Clutch size	90 to 110 eggs
Life span	Up to 50 years
Predators	Crabs, birds, fish (young only)

Diet The olive ridley sea turtle is mostly carnivorous. It feeds on jellyfish, snails, crabs and shrimp. They will occasionally eat algae and seaweed as well.

Fact These turtles lead solitary lives. Once a year, the females come together to lay their eggs on the beaches where they were hatched.

Conservation status **Vulnerable**

Common Snapping Turtle

Chelydra serpentina

Factfile

Habitat	Shallow ponds, shallow lakes, streams
Distribution	North America, Asia
Length	9 to 20 in (carapace length)
Clutch size	25 to 45 eggs
Life span	30 to 40 years
Predators	Birds, raccoons, snakes (young only)

Diet The common snapping turtle has a varied diet including plants, worms, leeches, snails, shrimp, crayfish, crabs, beetles, butterflies and carrion.

Fact Snapping turtles lay eggs which are the size of a Ping-Pong ball. The eggs hatch in early autumn. Not many of the babies survive to adulthood.

Conservation status **Least concern**

Leatherback Sea Turtle
Dermochelys coriacea

Factfile

Habitat	Open seas
Distribution	Worldwide
Length	Up to 5.5 ft (carapace length)
Clutch size	Up to 110 eggs
Life span	Up to 30 years
Predators	Orcas, sharks

Diet Leatherback sea turtles are carnivores. Their main prey are jellyfish and salps. They will also eat small crustaceans, sea urchins and snails.

Fact The leatherback sea turtle's esophagus is lined with short spines that prevent jellyfish from escaping from the turtle's open mouth once swallowed.

Conservation status

Chinese Soft-shelled Turtle

Pelodiscus sinensis

Factfile

Habitat	Rivers, lakes, ponds, creeks, marsh
Distribution	Asia
Length	Up to 12 in (carapace length)
Clutch size	8 to 30 eggs
Life span	Up to 60 years
Predators	Foxes, raccoons, dogs (eggs and young only)

Diet Chinese soft-shelled turtles eat fish, crustaceans, mollusks and insects. They will also eat some marsh plants but they are mostly carnivorous.

Fact In 2012 scientists discovered why these turtles submerge their heads in puddles. It is because they pass some urine through their mouths!

Conservation status   **Vulnerable**

Wood Turtle
Glyptemys insculpta

Factfile

Habitat	Streams, creeks, rivers
Distribution	North America
Length	6 to 10 in (carapace length)
Clutch size	3 to 20 eggs
Life span	Up to 60 years
Predators	Skunks, raccoons, dogs, cats

Diet The wood turtle's diet includes leaves, flowers, fruits, fungi, snails, worms and insects. They eat young mice or eggs, and scavenge dead animals.

Fact The oldest wood turtle fossil is an adult male specimen found in Nebraska. This fossil is believed to be around 6 million years old.

Conservation status   **Vulnerable**

Northern Map Turtle

Graptemys geographica

Factfile

Habitat	Rivers, streams
Distribution	North America
Length	8 to 11 in (carapace length)
Clutch size	6 to 20 eggs
Life span	5.5 years (in captivity)
Predators	Raccoons, coyotes, foxes, birds

Diet Northern map turtles hunt in water. They eat fish, snails and plants. Females also eat clams and crayfish. Males will eat insects and small crustaceans.

Fact Female northern map turtles are larger than the males and have more powerful jaws. This is why the males and females do not have exactly the same diet.

Conservation status   **Least concern**

Common Musk Turtle
Sternotherus odoratus

Factfile

Habitat	Lakes, ponds, rivers, streams
Distribution	North America
Length	3 to 5 in (carapace length)
Clutch size	2 to 9 eggs
Life span	Up to 54 years
Predators	Snakes, alligators, birds, skunks, raccoons

Diet The common musk turtle finds most of its food on the muddy bottom of streams or ponds. It eats plants, mollusks, small fish, insects and carrion.

Fact When disturbed, this turtle releases a smelly liquid from its musk glands. Because of this the turtle has been given the nickname "stinkpot."

Conservation status   **Least concern**

African Helmeted Turtle

Pelomedusa subrufa

Factfile

Habitat	Coast, marsh, creeks, rain holes
Distribution	Africa
Length	Up to 9 in (carapace length)
Clutch size	2 to 10 eggs
Life span	Up to 20 years
Predators	Foxes, mongooses

Diet The African helmeted turtle eats insects, small crustaceans, fish, earthworms and snails. They work together to catch larger prey such as doves.

Fact The African helmeted turtle is known for its foul smell. The aroma comes from glands under each leg that release a liquid that is repulsive to humans.

Conservation status   **Least concern**

Diamondback Terrapin
Malaclemys terrapin

Factfile

Habitat	Coast
Distribution	North America
Length	6 to 8 in (carapace length)
Clutch size	5 to 11 eggs
Life span	25 to 40 years
Predators	Raccoons prey on nesting females

Diet Diamondback terrapins eat crabs, snails and small bivalves, such as mussels and clams. They also eat carrion, fish, worms and insects.

Fact During the winter months, they hibernate in the mud at the bottom of creeks. They stay submerged and inactive throughout the winter.

Conservation status   **Near threatened**

Indian Star Tortoise

Geochelone elegans

Factfile

Habitat	Deserts, scrubland
Distribution	India, Sri Lanka
Length	6 to 12 in (carapace length)
Clutch size	1 to 10 eggs
Life span	35 to 80 years
Predators	Foxes, mongooses, hawks, vultures, reptiles

Diet The diet of the Indian star tortoise consists of herbaceous leaves, grasses, fruit and flowers. They will also eat insects, carrion and even some dung.

Fact During hot weather these tortoises are active only in the early morning and late afternoon. The rest of the day, they shelter under vegetation.

Conservation status   **Least concern**

Hermann's Tortoise

Testudo hermanni

Factfile

Habitat	Inland, coastal forest
Distribution	Western Europe
Length	Up to 8 in (carapace length)
Clutch size	2 to 12 eggs
Life span	Around 30 years
Predators	Rats, wild boars, birds, badgers, foxes, snakes

Diet Hermann's tortoises eat grasses, leaves and flowers. When vegetation is scarce, they will sometimes eat small insects, snails or slugs.

Fact These tortoises hibernate during the winter months. They usually hibernate under bushes or rotting wood, covering themselves with dead leaves.

Conservation status   **Near threatened**

Desert Tortoise

Gopherus agassizii

Reptiles

Turtles and tortoises

Tortoises

Factfile

Habitat	Desert, grassland, forest, mountains
Distribution	North America
Length	6 to 14 in (carapace length)
Clutch size	4 to 6 eggs
Life span	50 to 80 years
Predators	Pumas, foxes, coyotes, bobcats, eagles

Diet Desert tortoises survive on a diet of low-growing plants and freshly fallen leaves. They also eat bark, fruits, flowers, shrubs, stems and grasses.

Fact Desert tortoises dig catchment basins in the soil. When it eventually rains in the desert, the tortoise will return to these basins to drink.

Conservation status   **Vulnerable**

Leopard Tortoise
Stigmochelys pardalis

Factfile

Habitat	Desert, savannah, forest, mountains
Distribution	Africa
Length	12 to 28 in (carapace length)
Clutch size	5 to 18 eggs
Life span	Up to 100 years
Predators	Foxes, mongooses

Diet Leopard tortoises have a diet consisting of mixed grasses, succulents and thistles. They will also consume berries and other fruits when available.

Fact When threatened, these tortoises pull the head and legs into the shell. This action forces air from the lungs and creates a hissing noise.

Conservation status   **Not evaluated**

Texas Tortoise

Gopherus berlandieri

Factfile

Habitat	Semidesert, scrub forest
Distribution	North America
Length	Up to 9.5 in (carapace length)
Clutch size	2 to 3 eggs
Life span	25 to 60 years
Predators	Coyotes, birds, Gila monsters

Diet Grasses make up the majority of the Texas tortoise's diet along with herbs, wild flowers, and any rare fruits and berries that can be found.

Fact Nesting season is from April to July. The female lays a clutch of eggs in a hollow in the ground. Young tortoises will hatch after 88 to 118 days.

Conservation status **Vulnerable**

Gopher Tortoise

Gopherus polyphemus

Factfile

Habitat	Savannah, grassland, desert
Distribution	USA
Length	8 to 12 in (carapace length)
Clutch size	5 or 6 eggs
Life span	Up to 60 years
Predators	Possums, raccoons (eggs only)

Diet The gopher tortoise is a herbivore and forages for its food. It eats a diet of grasses and leaves, with occasional fruits and wild berries.

Fact Gopher tortoises dig burrows for shelter, which they share with other species. Animals that share shelters with other species are "keystone" species.

Conservation status   **Vulnerable**

Galápagos Tortoise

Chelonoidis nigra

Reptiles

Turtles and tortoises

Tortoises

Factfile

Habitat	Savannah, grasslands, forests
Distribution	Galápagos Islands
Length	Up to 44 in (carapace length)
Clutch size	Up to 16 eggs
Life span	Over 100 years
Predators	Rats, dogs, pigs (eggs and young only)

Diet Galápagos tortoises eat cactus, leaves, grass and berries. Cactus is one of their favorite foods. They can survive for a whole year without eating!

Fact Galápagos tortoises also eat poisonous fruit from the manchineel tree. These trees produce fruit that is so toxic it can kill humans.

Conservation status	Endangered

Northern Tuatara
Sphenodon punctatus

Factfile

Habitat	Coastal forests, pasture
Distribution	New Zealand and its surrounding islands
Length	16 to 24 in
Clutch size	5 to 18 eggs
Life span	35 to 60 years
Predators	Birds, cats, rats

Diet Adult tuatara usually hunt at night. They mostly eat insects, especially beetles, but have been known to eat lizards, birds and bird eggs.

Fact Tuatara mature slowly and are not fully grown until they are about 30 years old. They have a slow metabolism and can go for an hour without breathing.

Conservation status　　　**Least concern**

Amazon Tree Boa

Corallus hortulanus

Reptiles

Snakes and lizards

Snakes

Factfile

Habitat	Rain forest, savannah, dry forest
Distribution	Central and South America
Length	3.5 to 5 ft
Litter size	Up to 12 live young
Life span	Up to 20 years
Predators	Harpy eagles, saddleback tamarins

Diet Amazon tree boas have a broad diet consisting of mainly vertebrates. They will feed on birds, bats, frogs, rodents, lizards and marsupials.

Fact Amazon tree boas are viviparous, which means the female gives birth to live young rather than laying eggs that will later hatch.

Conservation status   Not evaluated

Boa Constrictor
Boa constrictor

Factfile

Habitat	Woodland, scrubland
Distribution	Central and South America
Length	Up to 13 ft
Litter size	10 to 64 live young
Life span	20 to 30 years
Predators	Jaguars, crocodiles, some large birds

Diet Boa constrictors are carnivorous snakes. They eat small mammals, including bats, and birds. However, they will sometimes eat larger animals.

Fact Boas are about 2 feet long when they are born and grow continually throughout their life span. The largest recorded boa constrictor was 18 feet.

Conservation status   **Not evaluated**

29

Emerald Tree Boa

Corallus caninus

Reptiles

Snakes and lizards

Snakes

Factfile

Habitat	Rain forest
Distribution	South America
Length	Up to 10 ft
Litter size	5 to 20 live young
Life span	Up to 15 years
Predators	Eagles

Diet The emerald tree boa's diet consists mostly of small mammals, such as rats, bats and possums, but it will also eat some birds and lizards.

Fact Emerald tree boas spend much of their time in the tree canopies. They are often found draped over branches in their signature looping coil.

Conservation status   Not evaluated

Green Anaconda

Eunectes murinus

Factfile

Habitat	Savannah, grassland, rain forest
Distribution	South America
Length	10 to 30 ft
Litter size	20 to 40 live young
Life span	Up to 10 years
Predators	Caimans, jaguars, other green anacondas

Diet The diet of the green anaconda consists of various aquatic and terrestrial vertebrates such as fish, reptiles, amphibians, birds and mammals.

Fact They detect prey using their sight, sensing vibrations, and using their forked tongues to taste the air for chemicals produced by animals.

Conservation status   **Not evaluated**

31

Rosy Boa
Charina trivirgata

Factfile

Habitat	Shrubland, desert, mountains
Distribution	USA, Mexico
Length	17 to 44 in
Litter size	1 to 14 live young
Life span	Up to 18 years
Predators	Raccoons, weasels, skunks, coyotes, birds

Diet The rosy boa's diet consists of small mammals such as rats, mice and baby rabbits. They will also eat some birds, amphibians and other reptiles.

Fact When under attack it will coil up leaving its head tucked into its body and its tail sticking out. A predator will attack the tail thinking it is the head.

Conservation status   **Least concern**

Burmese Python

Python molurus bivittatus

Factfile

Habitat	Grassland, swamp, woodland, rain forest
Distribution	Southeast Asia
Length	16 to 23 ft
Clutch size	Up to 100 eggs
Life span	20 to 25 years
Predators	No natural predators

Diet Burmese pythons prey on small mammals, up to the size of a pig or a small deer. They will also eat birds, lizards, other snakes, frogs and fish.

Fact Pythons wrap their bodies around prey. Each time the prey breathes out the snake tightens its grip. The prey is unable to inhale and soon dies.

Conservation status **Least concern**

Carpet Python
Morelia spilota

Factfile

Habitat	Rain forest, woodland, grassland, coast
Distribution	Australia, Indonesia, New Guinea
Length	6 to 12 ft
Clutch size	10 to 50 eggs
Life span	15 to 20 years
Predators	Birds of prey (young only)

Diet Carpet pythons can normally be seen feeding after dark. They primarily eat mammals and birds, although smaller pythons prefer to eat lizards.

Fact Pythons are primitive snakes who have "spurs" near the base of their tails. These spurs are leftover limbs that the species lost thousands of years ago.

Conservation status   **Least concern**

Reticulated Python
Python reticulatus

Factfile

Habitat	Tropical rain forest
Distribution	Southeast Asia
Length	Up to 30 ft
Clutch size	25 to 80 eggs
Life span	Up to 20 years
Predators	Humans

Diet Small reticulated pythons feed mostly on rats, but larger snakes will also eat bulkier mammals, such as porcupines, monkeys, wild pigs and dogs.

Fact The reticulated python is one of the largest snakes in the world. They swallow their prey whole and have occasionally been known to eat humans!

Conservation status   **Not evaluated**

Royal P thon
Python regius

Factfile

Habitat	Savannah, grassland, open forest
Distribution	West and Central Africa
Length	3 to 5 ft
Clutch size	1 to 11 eggs
Life span	Up to 10 years
Predators	Carnivores and birds of prey

Diet Royal pythons feed almost exclusively on rodents such as African giant rats, black rats, rufous-nosed rats, shaggy rats and grass mice.

Fact After laying her eggs, the female royal python coils her body around them to keep them at a steady temperature until they are ready to hatch.

Conservation status   **Least concern**

Mangrove Snake

Boiga dendrophila

Factfile

Habitat	Lowland rain forest, mangrove swamp
Distribution	Southeast Asia
Length	6 to 8 ft
Clutch size	4 to 8 eggs
Life span	Up to 17 years
Predators	Other snakes

Diet Young mangrove snakes will hunt for frogs, lizards and even large slugs, while large adults survive on a diet of small birds, reptiles and fish.

Fact Mangrove snakes are sometimes called gold-ringed cat snakes, due to their distinctive patterning: thin golden-yellow rings on a black background.

Conservation status   Not evaluated

Glossy Snake

Arizona elegans

Factfile

Habitat	Savannah, grassland, desert, forest
Distribution	USA and Mexico
Length	2.5 to 6 ft
Clutch size	Up to 23 eggs
Life span	4 to 25 years
Predators	Owls, mammals, other snakes

Diet Around half the diet of the glossy snake is made up of other reptiles, while the rest is made up of small mammals such mice, rats and moles.

Fact This nocturnal ground-dweller is a burrower that spends most of its time underground. It hibernates for the winter in an underground burrow.

Conservation status Not evaluated

Eastern Racer
Coluber constrictor

Factfile

Habitat	Savannah, grasslands, marsh
Distribution	The Americas
Length	2 to 6 ft
Clutch size	3 to 32 eggs
Life span	Up to 10 years
Predators	Birds, dogs, cats, coyotes

Diet Young eastern racers eat insects, spiders, frogs and reptiles, while adults eat birds, eggs, small rodents, toads, lizards, and other snakes.

Fact Despite its common name, the racer's actual speed is about 4 miles per hour which is only about as fast as a human walking briskly.

Conservation status   **Least concern**

39

Boomslang
Dispholidus typus

Factfile

Habitat	Savannah, grassland, scrubland
Distribution	Africa
Length	4 to 7 ft
Clutch size	Up to 30 eggs
Life span	Up to 8 years
Predators	Large snakes, birds of prey

Diet The diet of the boomslang consists of small lizards and frogs. Occasionally, they feed on small mammals, birds, eggs, and even other boomslangs.

Fact Boomslangs hunt in trees and shrubs. They glide over branches to find a hiding place. They capture most of their prey without being seen.

Conservation status   **Not evaluated**

Eastern Indigo Snake

Drymarchon couperi

Factfile

Habitat	Savannah, grassland, desert, forest
Distribution	USA
Length	5 to 7 ft
Clutch size	4 to 12 eggs
Life span	12 to 21 years
Predators	Hawks (young only)

Diet Eastern indigo snakes have a varied diet. They eat mammals, frogs, lizards, fish, eggs, birds and snakes, including some venomous ones.

Fact Eastern indigo snakes are often found living in burrows with gopher tortoises. The snakes take shelter in the burrows that the tortoise has dug.

Conservation status	**Least concern**

Blunthead Tree Snake

Imantodes cenchoa

Factfile

Habitat	Forest
Distribution	Central America
Length	25 to 35 in
Clutch size	1 to 3 eggs
Life span	Estimated at 10 to 20 years
Predators	Birds of prey

Diet Blunthead tree snakes forage at night. They eat a variety of prey, including small tree-dwelling lizards and frogs, as well as frog and reptile eggs.

Fact The blunthead tree snake's head is very large in comparision to its slender body. Its eyes are very large, protruding with slit-like, vertical pupils.

Conservation status   **Not evaluated**

Common Kingsnake

Lampropeltis getula

Factfile

Habitat	Desert, savannah, forest, mountains
Distribution	North America
Length	2 to 5 ft
Clutch size	3 to 24 eggs
Life span	Up to 9 years
Predators	Alligators, hawks, raccoons, skunks, snakes

Diet Common kingsnakes feed on other snakes, including coral snakes, copperheads and rattlesnakes. They also eat some skinks and mice.

Fact Common kingsnakes kill and eat venomous snakes. They are immune to pit-viper venom, so a bite from a venomous snake has little effect.

Conservation status   **Least concern**

43

Milk Snake

Lampropeltis triangulum

Factfile

Habitat	Savannah, grassland, forest
Distribution	North and Central America
Length	2 to 4.5 ft
Clutch size	2 to 17 eggs
Life span	Up to 20 years
Predators	Raccoons, foxes, skunks, coyotes

Diet The milk snake has a diet of mostly rodents such as voles, mice and rats. They will also eat birds, bird eggs, lizards, snake eggs and other snakes.

Fact Milk snakes lay their eggs in rotting logs or moist, warm leaf litter. They hatch after a month as young milk snakes that are 5.5 to 11 inches long.

Conservation status	**Not evaluated**

Coachwhip
Masticophis flagellum

Factfile

Habitat	Savannah, grassland, forest
Distribution	USA, Mexico
Length	4 to 7 ft
Clutch size	4 to 16 eggs
Life span	Up to 20 years
Predators	Hawks, roadrunners

Diet The coachwhip eats birds, rodents, lizards, other snakes, small turtles, bird eggs and insects. It often eats several rodents during one feeding.

Fact These snakes are said to resemble whips because they are so slender. They have a very thin head, so it can be difficult to tell the head from the tail.

Conservation status   **Least concern**

Northern Water Snake

Nerodia sipedon

Factfile

Habitat	Rivers and streams, ponds, lakes
Distribution	USA
Length	2 to 4.5 ft
Litter size	4 to 99 live young
Life span	Up to 9 years
Predators	Large snakes, raccoons, skunks, foxes

Diet Northern water snakes eat a variety of prey, such as amphibians, fish, crayfish, large insects, leeches, other snakes, turtles and birds.

Fact Northern water snakes repeatedly strike any attackers. Their saliva contains a substance that stops blood from clotting easily.

Conservation status   **Least concern**

Rough Green Snake
Opheodrys aestivus

Factfile

Habitat	Forest edges near ponds or lakes
Distribution	North America
Length	2 to 3 ft
Clutch size	3 to 12 eggs
Life span	Up to 5 years
Predators	Snakes, birds, domestic cats

Diet Rough green snakes are insectivores. They use their superb vision to hunt for crickets, grasshoppers, caterpillars, spiders and moths.

Fact They are called "rough" as their scales stand out at a slight angle. They are skilled climbers, and are often found on bushes, vines and trees.

Conservation status **Least concern**

Smooth Green Snake

Opheodrys vernalis

Factfile

Habitat	Savannah, grassland, forest
Distribution	USA and Canada
Length	1 to 2 ft
Clutch size	3 to 13 eggs
Life span	Up to 6 years
Predators	Hawks, crows, raccoons, foxes, snakes

Diet Most of the smooth green snake's diet is insects such as crickets, grasshoppers and beetles. They also eat snails, caterpillars and amphibians.

Fact The snake's green skin is a combination of blue and yellow pigment. When it dies, the yellow pigment fades, leaving the dead snake a blue color.

Conservation status   **Least concern**

Green Vine Snake

Oxybelis fulgidus

Factfile

Habitat	Rain forest
Distribution	The Americas
Length	5 to 6.5 ft
Clutch size	5 to 12 eggs
Life span	Up to 15 years
Predators	Birds, large mammals

Diet The green vine snake eats birds, especially hummingbirds. It will position itself by a flower and remain motionless, waiting for hummingbirds to approach.

Fact They use camouflage to hide from predators and to ambush their prey. The green color of their skin blends in with vines and branches.

Conservation status **Not evaluated**

Red Corn Snake

Pantherophis guttatus

Factfile

Habitat	Savannah, grassland, forest
Distribution	North America
Length	2 to 6 ft
Clutch size	10 to 15 eggs
Life span	Up to 32 years
Predators	Other snakes

Diet Red corn snakes eat every few days. Half of their diet consists of rodents such as rats and mice. They also eat other small mammals such as moles.

Fact When shedding skin a corn snake rubs its nose on rocks to loosen the skin, then it slithers forward and the skin slides off in one long piece.

Conservation status　　　**Least concern**

Eastern Fox Snake
Pantherophis gloydi

Factfile

Habitat   Savannah, grassland, marsh, lakes and ponds
Distribution   USA
Length   3 to 4.5 ft
Clutch size   7 to 29 eggs
Life span   25 to 30 years
Predators   Egrets, herons, hawks, raccoons, foxes

Diet   Eastern fox snakes feed on small mammals, particularly meadow voles and deer mice. They will also eat earthworms, eggs, insects and frogs.

Fact   Eastern fox snakes are constrictors. They kill by wrapping their bodies around their prey and slowly squeezing until the prey cannot breathe and dies.

Conservation status   **Near threatened**

Yellow Rat Snake

Elaphe obsoleta quadrivittata

Factfile

Habitat	Savannah, grassland, forest
Distribution	USA
Length	3 to 6 ft
Clutch size	12 to 20 eggs
Life span	Up to 20 years
Predators	Raccoons, foxes, bobcats, owls, hawks

Diet Although yellow rat snakes are known as rodent eaters, they eat a variety of prey. Young rat snakes will often eat lizards and small frogs.

Fact Yellow rat snakes are very useful around barns and in farming communities because they lower populations of pests such as mice and rats.

Conservation status   **Least concern**

Queen Snake
Regina septemvittata

Factfile

Habitat	Rivers and streams, ponds and lakes
Distribution	North America
Length	14 to 36 in
Litter size	5 to 23 live young
Life span	Up to 19 years
Predators	Herons, raccoons, mink, snakes large frogs

Diet Queen snakes eat some fish and tadpoles, but mostly eat crayfish, preferring ones that have recently molted their hard exoskeletons.

Fact The queen snake is a very good swimmer. It shelters under partially submerged rocks and pieces of wood, along the edge of a stream.

Conservation status   Least concern

Pine Woods Snake

Rhadinaea flavilata

Factfile

Habitat	Woodland
Distribution	USA
Length	10 to 12 in
Clutch size	2 to 4 eggs
Life span	Up to 3 years
Predators	Other snakes

Diet The pine woods snake is generally only likely to eat small animals, with lizards and frogs being among the main prey. It will occasionally eat small snakes.

Fact Pine woods snakes are burrowers. They are often found in dens in rotting logs or under piles of leaves. If uncovered, they scurry for shelter.

Conservation status   **Least concern**

Dekay's Brown Snake

Storeria dekayi

Factfile

Habitat	Forest, scrubland, woodland, marsh
Distribution	North America
Length	9 to 15 in
Litter size	12 to 20 live young
Life span	Up to 7 years
Predators	Frogs, toads, snakes, birds, shrews, cats

Diet Dekay's brown snakes feed predominately on earthworms, snails and slugs. They will also eat soft-bodied grubs, beetles and small salamanders.

Fact Dekay's brown snakes are grayish-brown in color with a lighter streak on the back that is bordered with black dots and a pinkish-white belly.

Conservation status   **Least concern**

Wandering Garter Snake

Thamnophis elegans vagrans

Reptiles

Snakes and lizards

Snakes

Factfile

Habitat	Grassland, forest
Distribution	North America
Length	6 to 30 in
Litter size	Up to 20 live young
Life span	Up to 9 years
Predators	Kingsnakes, bullfrogs, sunfish

Diet Wandering garter snakes eat slugs, small mammals and fish. They will sometimes feed on amphibians, leeches, birds and even other snakes.

Fact When threatened, the wandering garter snake sometimes discharges a foul-smelling musk from glands at the base of its tail to deter attackers.

Conservation status   **Not evaluated**

Butler's Garter Snake

Thamnophis butleri

Factfile

Habitat	Savannah, grassland, forest
Distribution	North America
Length	15 to 30 in
Litter size	4 to 14 live young
Life span	Up to 12 years
Predators	Birds, raccoons, skunks, foxes, snakes

Diet The Butler's garter snake has a diet that is mostly made up of earthworms, but they will also eat leeches, small frogs and some salamanders.

Fact Butler's garter snakes are mostly solitary, though they will congregate together with other garter snakes when they hibernate underground.

Conservation status   **Least concern**

Common Garter Snake

Thamnophis sirtalis

Reptiles

Snakes and lizards

Snakes

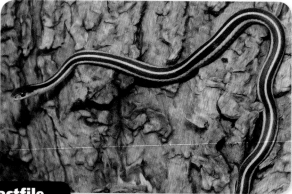

Factfile

Habitat	Grassland, marsh, woodland, hillsides
Distribution	North America
Length	1.5 to 4.5 ft
Litter size	12 to 40 live young
Life span	Up to 20 years
Predators	Turtles, raccoons, foxes, squirrels, shrews

Diet The common garter snake eats frogs, earthworms, fish, tadpoles, voles, salamanders and even young birds. It always swallows its prey alive.

Fact The common garter snake loves to eat earthworms. They make up a big part of its diet and the snake can eat up to 14 earthworms per hour!

Conservation status   Least concern

Plains Garter Snake

Thamnophis radix

Factfile

Habitat   Savannah, grassland, ponds, streams
Distribution North America
Length   16 to 28 in
Litter size   5 to 60 live young
Life span   Up to 8 years
Predators   Hawks, kestrels, foxes, coyotes, skunks

Diet Plains garter snakes have a varied diet of frogs and toads, fish, salamanders, birds, leeches, small rodents, earthworms and some grasshoppers.

Fact To discourage predators attacking them, these snakes will hide their heads, coil up their bodies and emit a foul-smelling musk.

Conservation status   **Least concern**

Eastern Ribbon Snake
Thamnophis sauritus

Factfile

Habitat	Savannah, grassland, marsh, lakes, ponds
Distribution	North and Central America
Length	1.5 to 3 ft
Litter size	4 to 27 live young
Life span	Up to 10 years
Predators	Herons, hawks, mink, raccoons, fish, bullfrogs

Diet Eastern ribbon snakes have a diet consisting mainly of frogs, salamanders and their larvae. They will also eat small fish and occasionally earthworms.

Fact The eastern ribbon snake is semiaquatic, living in wet areas near water. Even though it is a good swimmer it prefers the shore to open water.

Conservation status　　　　**Least concern**

60

Lined Snake

Tropidoclonion lineatum

Factfile

Habitat	Savannah, grassland, forest
Distribution	USA
Length	8.5 to 15 in
Litter size	2 to 12 live young
Life span	3 to 10 years
Predators	Birds, some mammals

Diet Lined snakes mainly feed on earthworms, but will also eat some bugs, snails, soft-bodied insects and slugs. They forage at night or after rain.

Fact The body of the lined snake varies from olive to gray-brown. The stripe down the middle of the back varies from white to orange.

Conservation status   **Not evaluated**

Black Mamba

Dendroaspis polylepis

Factfile

Habitat	Savannah, grassland, forest
Distribution	Africa
Length	7 to 9 ft
Clutch size	6 to 18 eggs
Life span	Up to 11 years
Predators	Birds, crocodiles, mongooses, foxes, jackals

Diet Black mambas feed mostly on small mammals, such as rodents, squirrels or hyraxes. They have occasionally been observed eating birds.

Fact Black mambas will strike once or twice, injecting venom. The venom paralyzes and kills the prey. The snake then swallows the prey whole.

Conservation status   **Least concern**

Eastern Green Mamba

Dendroaspis angusticeps

Factfile

Habitat	Forest, coastal scrub, woodland, savannah
Distribution	Africa
Length	4.5 to 7 ft
Clutch size	6 to 17 eggs
Life span	Up to 11 years
Predators	Other snakes, crocodiles, mongooses, foxes

Diet Eastern green mambas pursue their prey, striking rapidly until the prey succumbs to the venom. They eat birds, bats, eggs and small mammals.

Fact The slender eastern green mamba is persistently arboreal, meaning it lives in trees, and only occasionally descends to forage on the ground.

Conservation status   **Not evaluated**

63

Eastern Coral Snake

Micrurus fulvius

Factfile

Habitat	Forest
Distribution	USA, Mexico
Length	Up to 2.5 ft
Clutch size	5 to 7 eggs
Life span	Up to 6 years
Predators	Kingsnakes, kestrels, hawks

Diet Eastern coral snakes mostly eat other snakes, including their own species. They will also feed on lizards, birds, frogs, fish and some insects.

Fact When an eastern coral snake feels threatened it will curl the tip of its tail. This action is done to confuse the attacker as to which end is its head.

Conservation status   **Least concern**

64

Egyptian Cobra

Naja haje

Factfile

Habitat	Savannah, woodland, grassland, desert
Distribution	Africa
Length	6 to 8 ft
Clutch size	8 to 88 eggs
Life span	Up to 20 years
Predators	Mongooses, honey badgers

Diet Egyptian cobras especially enjoy eating toads, but they also feed on mammals, birds, eggs, lizards, snakes, frogs and sometimes fish.

Fact Egyptian cobras, like all cobras, have elongated ribs that can extend the skin on the neck to create a hood. This makes the snake look bigger.

Conservation status Not evaluated

King Cobra

Ophiophagus hannah

Factfile

Habitat	Savannah, grassland, forest, scrubland
Distribution	Asia
Length	10 to 12 ft
Clutch size	20 to 40 eggs
Life span	Up to 20 years
Predators	Mongooses, army ants (young only), birds of prey

Diet The king cobra mostly eats other snakes. It usually preys on larger nonvenomous species, such as Asian rat snakes and pythons up to 10 feet in length.

Fact Adult king cobras are yellow, green, brown or black. Usually there are yellow or white crossbars on the body. The throat is yellow or cream.

Conservation status   **Vulnerable**

Southern Copperhead
Agkistrodon contortrix

Factfile

Habitat	Wetland
Distribution	USA
Length	Up to 40 in
Litter size	2 to 10 live young
Life span	Up to 30 years
Predators	Other snakes, birds of prey

Diet The southern copperhead is a carnivore. It has a diet mostly consisting of mice but also some birds, lizards, amphibians and insects.

Fact Young copperheads are grayer in color than adults. They have a sulphur-yellow-tipped tail, which fades with age and is lost by age 3 or 4.

Conservation status   **Least concern**

African Bush Viper

Atheris squamigera

Reptiles

Snakes and lizards

Snakes

Factfile

Habitat	Tropical forest
Distribution	Central and Western Africa
Length	20 to 30 in
Litter size	2 to 19 live young
Life span	10 to 20 years
Predators	Other snakes

Diet African bush vipers do most of their hunting at night. They feed on shrews and rodents. They will also eat some birds and small reptiles.

Fact All vipers are ovoviviparous. This means that after gestation, eggs hatch inside the mother's body, where they complete their development.

Conservation status	Not evaluated

68

Eyelash Viper

Bothriechis schlegelii

Factfile

Habitat	Forest, rain forest
Distribution	The Americas
Length	14 to 32 in
Litter size	6 to 20 live young
Life span	Up to 10 years
Predators	Hedgehogs, badgers, foxes, cats

Diet The eyelash viper feeds on a wide variety of small vertebrate animals, such as frogs, lizards, birds, bats, rodents and marsupials.

Fact The scales over the eyes of the eyelash viper give the appearance of eyelashes. Individuals are found in different colors such as yellow, green and pink.

Conservation status	Not evaluated

Gaboon Viper

Bitis gabonica

Factfile

Habitat	Rain forest, woodland, grassland
Distribution	Northwest and East Africa
Length	4 to 6 ft
Litter size	30 to 40 live young
Life span	Up to 18 years
Predators	No known predators

Diet Gaboon vipers mostly eat small mammals, birds, frogs and toads. Some have been known to eat giant rats, porcupines and even antelopes.

Fact Gaboon vipers lie still, blending in with the leaves of the forest floor, waiting for prey to cross their path. They are most active around sunset.

Conservation status   **Not evaluated**

Rhinoceros Viper

Bitis nasicornis

Factfile

Habitat	Tropical forest
Distribution	Central and Western Africa
Length	2 to 3 ft
Litter size	6 to 35 live young
Life span	Up to 8 years
Predators	Other snakes

Diet The rhinoceros viper uses camouflage to hide from its prey. It mainly hunts for small mammals, but will also eat some amphibians and fish.

Fact This viper's head is flat, triangular and small compared to the rest of its body. There are two or three hornlike scales above each nostril.

Conservation status   **Least concern**

Western Diamondback

Crotalus atrox

Factfile

Habitat	Desert, savannah, grassland
Distribution	North and Central America
Length	Up to 6.5 ft
Litter size	Up to 14 live young
Life span	Up to 20 years
Predators	Birds of prey, coyotes, foxes

Diet The western diamondback is a rattlesnake that preys on small mammals and birds. It will also eat reptiles, fish, amphibians and invertebrates.

Fact These diamondbacks use their rattles to distract prey and to warn off predators. The rattle is made from old dry skin that does not shed.

Conservation status   **Least concern**

Eastern Diamondback

Crotalus adamanteus

Factfile

Habitat	Forests
Distribution	USA
Length	2.5 to 6 ft
Litter size	6 to 21 live young
Life span	Up to 20 years
Predators	Eagles, hawks, badgers, kingsnakes

Diet The eastern diamondback feeds mostly on mammals, ranging in size from mice to rabbits. They will also catch and eat the occasional bird.

Fact These rattlesnakes often take refuge in the burrows of other animals, and will also use holes in stumps, logs, and other underground cavities.

Conservation status   **Least concern**

Massasauga Rattlesnake

Sistrurus catenatus

Factfile

Habitat	Forest, swamp, marsh, wet prairies
Distribution	North America
Length	1.5 to 3.5 ft
Little size	3 to 19 live young
Life span	Up to 20 years
Predators	Snakes, hawks, herons, raccoons, foxes

Diet The massasauga rattlesnake has a diet of mostly small mammals such as voles, mice and shrews. They will also eat frogs, birds and other snakes.

Fact The massasauga rattlesnake has many names, such as the black rattler, sauger, black massasauga, swamp rattler, or the gray rattlesnake.

Conservation status   **Least concern**

Mojave Rattlesnake

Crotalus scutulatus

Factfile

Habitat	Desert, grassland, scrubland
Distribution	USA, Mexico
Length	3 to 4.5 ft
Litter size	2 to 17 live young
Life span	Up to 24 years
Predators	Hawks, eagles, coyotes, other snakes

Diet Mojave rattlesnakes feed on rats, mice, lizards, birds and frogs. They use venom injected through long, hollow, retractable fangs to kill.

Fact The mojave rattlesnake is widely considered the most toxic rattlesnake in the USA. One bite could kill an adult human if left untreated.

Conservation status　　　**Least concern**

75

Prairie Rattlesnake

Crotalus viridis

Reptiles

Snakes and lizards

Snakes

Factfile

Habitat	Savannah, grassland, forest
Distribution	North America
Length	3.5 to 4 ft
Litter size	4 to 12 live young
Life span	Up to 25 years
Predators	Birds of prey

Diet Prairie rattlesnakes have a diet consisting of small mammals, amphibians, ground nesting birds, and reptiles, including other species of snakes.

Fact Prairie rattlesnakes hunt in the daytime during spring and autumn. During the hot summer they shelter in the daytime and hunt at night.

Conservation status **Least concern**

Tiger Rattlesnake

Crotalus tigris

Factfile

Habitat	Desert, savannah, grassland
Distribution	USA
Length	1.5 to 3 ft
Litter size	1 to 6 live young
Life span	Estimated at 10 to 20 years
Predators	Hawks, eagles, coyotes, other snakes

Diet Tiger rattlesnakes are carnivores who inject their prey with deadly venom. They mostly feed on lizards and small mammals such as mice and rats.

Fact Rattlesnakes have fangs that lie parallel to the jaw when not in use. The tiger rattlesnake's fangs are shorter than those of most other rattlesnakes.

Conservation status   **Least concern**

Timber Rattlesnake

Crotalus horridus

Factfile

Habitat	Forest, mountains
Distribution	North America
Length	3 to 5 ft
Litter size	Up to 20 live young
Life span	Up to 30 years
Predators	Hawks, bobcats, coyotes, foxes, skunks

Diet The main diet of the timber rattlesnake is small mammals, in particular mice, rats, squirrels, and rabbits. Birds are also sometimes killed and eaten.

Fact Large groups of timber rattlesnakes will hibernate together during the winter. Other species of snakes may hibernate with them.

Conservation status   **Least concern**

Puff Adder
Bitis arietans

Factfile

Habitat	Arid regions, swamps, dense forest
Distribution	Africa
Length	4 to 6 ft
Litter size	50 to 60 live young
Life span	Up to 14 years
Predators	Honey badgers, warthogs, birds of prey, snakes

Diet The puff adder is known to feed on a variety of animals. Their diet consists mainly of rodents, but birds, lizards and toads are also included.

Fact The puff adder is considered to be a highly dangerous snake. It is responsible for most of the lethal snake bites that happen in Africa.

Conservation status	**Not evaluated**

Common European Adder

Vipera berus

Reptiles

Snakes and lizards

Snakes

Factfile

Habitat	Savannah, grassland, forest
Distribution	Europe and Asia
Length	6.5 to 32 in
Litter size	Up to 20 live young
Life span	Up to 10 years
Predators	Foxes, badgers, birds of prey, owls, snakes

Diet The common European adder eats small mammals such as voles, shrews and mice. It will also eat some small lizards, birds and frogs.

Fact Adders wait for prey to pass by, then they strike out, injecting the prey with venom. When the prey has died the adder will swallow it head first.

Conservation status   **Least concern**

Frilled Lizard

Chlamydosaurus kingii

Factfile

Habitat	Subtropical woodland
Distribution	Australia
Length	Up to 33 in
Clutch size	4 to 13 eggs
Life span	Up to 10 years
Predators	Birds of prey, larger lizards, snakes, dingoes

Diet Frilled lizards have a diet that is largely made up of insects, but they have been known to eat small mammals and pieces of meat from time to time.

Fact When this lizard is threatened it opens the leathery frill around its neck. The frill is often brightly colored and makes the lizard look larger.

Conservation status   **Least concern**

81

Thorny Devil

Moloch horridus

Factfile

Habitat	Desert, scrubland
Distribution	Australia
Length	Up to 8 in
Clutch size	3 to 10 eggs
Life span	6 to 20 years
Predators	Australian bustards, buzzards, large lizards

Diet Thorny devils only eat ants. Ants are quite low in nutrients so the lizard needs to consume huge quantities. It is believed they eat 750 ants daily.

Fact In between the spikes on the thorny devil, little channels form, enabling the lizard to move any water collected on its body to its mouth.

Conservation status   **Not evaluated**

Asian Water Dragon

Physignathus cocincinus

Factfile

Habitat	Forest, jungle
Distribution	Asia
Length	24 to 40 in
Clutch size	5 to 15 eggs
Life span	10 to 20 years
Predators	Birds, snakes, mammals

Diet Asian water dragons eat a variety of plant and animal species. They prey upon small animals such as lizards, frogs, rodents, insects and fish.

Fact Water dragons are strong and capable swimmers and often leap into the water from the branches high above in order to escape approaching danger.

Conservation status   Not evaluated

Slow Worm
Anguis fragilis

Factfile

Habitat	Forest, farmland, desert, grassland
Distribution	Asia, Europe
Length	Up to 20 in
Litter size	2 live young
Life span	Up to 30 years
Predators	Cats, dogs, birds

Diet Slow worms are carnivores. They are often found in grass and damp environments where they are likely to find their prey of slugs and worms.

Fact Although slow worms look like snakes, they are in fact legless lizards. An easy way to tell them apart is that lizards have eyelids while snakes do not.

Conservation status   **Least concern**

Madrean Alligator Lizard
Elgaria kingii

Factfile

Habitat   Desert, grassland, woodland
Distribution   North America
Length   Up to 5.5 in
Clutch size   Up to 15 eggs
Life span   Up to 10 years
Predators   Snakes

Diet The madrean alligator lizard eats a variety of insects, including grasshoppers, caterpillars and moths. It also occasionally eats scorpions.

Fact Like many lizards, the madrean alligator lizard is able to drop its tail when threatened by predators. The tail will regenerate at a later time.

Conservation status   **Least concern**

Iberian Worm Lizard

Blanus cinereus

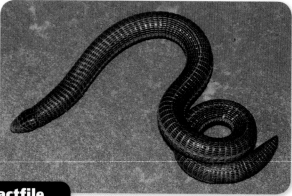

Factfile

Habitat	Moist, sandy soil
Distribution	Europe, North Africa
Length	Up to 12 in
Clutch size	1 or 2 eggs
Life span	Up to 16 years
Predators	Wild boar, genets, foxes, buzzards, snakes

Diet
Iberian worm lizards use their forked tongues to "taste" for chemicals in the air in order to find their prey of beetles, earthworms and ant larvae.

Fact
The skin of the Iberian worm lizard is loose fitting and segmented like an earthworm, but each of the rings consists of tiny squarish scales.

Conservation status   **Least concern**

Common Collared Lizard

Crotaphytus collaris

Factfile

Habitat	Rocky areas, woodland, grassland
Distribution	North America
Length	8 to 14 in
Clutch size	Up to 12 eggs
Life span	Up to 10 years
Predators	Eagles, snakes

Diet Occasionally the common collared lizard will eat some plant matter, although the bulk of its diet is made up of insects and smaller lizards.

Fact The common collared lizard is known for running rapidly upright on its hind legs. It also waves its tail in a cat-like fashion before grabbing prey.

Conservation status   **Least concern**

Armadillo Girdled Lizard

Cordylus cataphractus

Reptiles

Snakes and lizards

Lizards

Factfile

Habitat	Desert, semidesert
Distribution	South Africa
Length	6 to 8 in
Litter size	1 to 2 live young
Life span	Up to 20 years
Predators	Birds of prey

Diet In springtime the armadillo girdled lizard feasts on termites. For the rest of the year it eats beetles, millipedes, scorpions and plant material.

Fact When under attack this lizard takes its tail in its mouth and rolls into a ball. In this shape it is protected from predators by its thick, squarish scales.

Conservation status   **Vulnerable**

Parson's Chameleon
Calumma parsonii

Factfile

Habitat	Forest
Distribution	Madagascar
Length	17 to 27 in
Clutch size	20 to 25 eggs
Life span	3 to 8 years
Predators	Birds, snakes, mammals

Diet Parson's chameleons are nonvenomous and primarily survive by eating small as well as large insects. They will also eat some small vertebrates.

Fact The Parson's chameleon can change its skin color to regulate temperature, communicate with others, and camouflage against predators.

Conservation status   **Near threatened**

Jackson's Chameleon

Chamaeleo jacksonii

Reptiles

Snakes and lizards

Lizards

Factfile

Habitat	Rain forest
Distribution	East Africa
Length	6 to 14 in
Litter size	8 to 30 live young
Life span	3 to 8 years
Predators	Birds, snakes, shrews, lizards

Diet Jackson's chameleons have a varied diet of lizards, snails, caterpillars, amphibians and plant matter, including leaves, berries and shoots.

Fact The tongue of the Jackson's chameleon is one and a half times the lizard's length. It can be projected to full length in just a sixteenth of a second.

Conservation status   **Not evaluated**

Carpet Chameleon
Furcifer lateralis

Factfile

Habitat	Savannah, grassland, forest, scrubland
Distribution	Madagascar
Length	7 to 10 in
Clutch size	8 to 23 eggs
Life span	Up to 3 years
Predators	Snakes, birds

Diet
The carpet chameleon is almost entirely insectivorous. It enjoys a diet that includes grasshoppers, crickets, flies, and various insect larvae.

Fact
Carpet chameleons follow the same routine every day. Some chameleons have even been observed sleeping on the same branch every night.

Conservation status   Least concern

Panther Chameleon

Furcifer pardalis

Factfile

Habitat	Tropical forest, coastal lowland
Distribution	Madagascar
Length	9 to 20 in
Clutch size	10 to 40 eggs
Life span	1 to 3 years
Predators	Birds, snakes

Diet Panther chameleons wait for prey to pass within range of their long tongues. They feed mostly on invertebrates and some plant material.

Fact Chameleons use their long sticky tongues to capture prey. They shoot their tongues out and make a "suction cup" shape at the end to capture prey.

Conservation status   **Least concern**

Veiled Chameleon
Chamaeleo calyptratus

Factfile

Habitat	Desert, forest, mountains
Distribution	Yemen, Saudi Arabia
Length	17 to 24 in
Clutch size	35 to 85 eggs
Life span	Up to 8 years
Predators	Birds, snakes, lizards

Diet The veiled chameleon eats a variety of insects. It is one of the few chameleons that will also eat plants. They eat the leaves to gain water.

Fact When startled they curl into a tight position, darken in color, and play dead. It takes quite a lot of time until they feel secure enough to unfold.

Conservation status   **Least concern**

93

Crested Gecko

Rhacodactylus ciliatus

Reptiles

Snakes and lizards

Lizards

Factfile

Habitat	Rain forest
Distribution	New Caledonia
Length	Up to 8 in
Clutch size	2 eggs
Life span	10 to 20 years
Predators	Dogs, cats, rats, snakes, lizards, insects

Diet Crested geckos are omnivores, meaning they eat plant and animal material. They feed on insects, nectar and fruits. They hunt and feed at night.

Fact One of the main predators of this gecko are fire ants. They swarm the gecko, stinging and attacking, then eat the dead gecko's body.

Conservation status   **Not evaluated**

94

Common Leopard Gecko

Eublepharis macularius

Factfile

Habitat	Desert, grassland
Distribution	Asia
Length	8 to 11 in
Clutch size	2 eggs
Life span	Up to 4 years
Predators	Snakes, frogs, foxes, large reptiles

Diet Common leopard geckos will eat just about any moving creature that is smaller than themselves, including insects, spiders, snails and scorpions.

Fact Like all reptiles, leopard geckos shed their skin. Adults do this about once a month. Once shed, the leopard gecko will eat its old skin.

Conservation status   **Not evaluated**

Tokay Gecko

Gekko gecko

Factfile

Habitat	Forests, buildings
Distribution	Asia, Caribbean, North America
Length	Up to 16 in
Clutch size	2 eggs
Life span	Up to 10 years
Predators	Snakes

Diet Like most geckos, tokays hunt insects. They eat a variety including locusts, crickets and cockroaches, as well as centipedes and scorpions.

Fact Tokay geckos eat pests such as cockroaches and locusts. In parts of Asia, they are regarded as bringing good luck, fortune and fertility.

Conservation status   **Not evaluated**

Web-footed Gecko

Pachydactylus rangei

Factfile

Habitat	Desert
Distribution	Africa
Length	4 to 6 in
Clutch size	2 eggs
Life span	1 to 5 years
Predators	Namib golden moles, owls, snakes

Diet The web-footed gecko has a diet that consists of small spiders, grasshoppers and any arthropod small enough for the lizard to digest.

Fact The web-footed gecko hunts at night when most insects are active. Their large eyes and vertical pupils help them see well in the darkness of night.

Conservation status   **Not evaluated**

Turkish Gecko

Hemidactylus turcicus

Reptiles

Snakes and lizards

Lizards

Factfile

Habitat	European Mediterranean coast
Distribution	Morocco, Portugal, Jordan, Turkey, Egypt
Length	Up to 6 in
Clutch size	2 eggs
Life span	Up to 8 years
Predators	Bats, some insects, large spiders, cats

Diet The Turkish gecko feeds on spiders, insects and certain kinds of small invertebrates. They hunt at night when most of their prey are active.

Fact Their feet are unique by having adhesive pads, which do not extend to the toe tips, to aid climbing. Their scientific name means "half-finger" in Latin.

Conservation status   Least concern

Gila Monster
Heloderma suspectum

Factfile

Habitat	Desert
Distribution	North America
Length	Up to 22 in
Clutch size	2 to 12 eggs
Life span	20 to 30 years
Predators	Coyotes, birds of prey

Diet The Gila monster has the capability to eat huge amounts of food at one time. It feeds on mice, rabbits, squirrels, birds, lizards and eggs.

Fact Gila monsters live underground, emerging only to feed or bask in the sun. They store fat in their tails and can go for months between meals.

Conservation status   **Near threatened**

Marine Iguana

Amblyrhynchus cristatus

Reptiles

Snakes and lizards

Lizards

Factfile

Habitat	Coast, shallow coastal seas
Distribution	Galápagos Islands
Length	2.5 to 5 ft
Clutch size	1 to 6 eggs
Life span	5 to 12 years
Predators	Hawks, owls, snakes, crabs, rats, dogs, cats

Diet
Adult marine iguanas dive for food in the cold waters off the Galápagos Islands. They can dive down to 40 feet to find the algae and seaweed.

Fact
Some marine iguanas have learned that when a mockingbird lets out a certain cry, it means hawks are around and they should run for cover.

Conservation status **Vulnerable**

Common Green Iguana

Iguana iguana

Factfile

Habitat	Forest, mangrove
Distribution	Central and South America, Caribbean, Hawaii
Length	Up to 6.5 ft
Clutch size	Up to 65 eggs
Life span	Up to 20 years
Predators	Birds of prey

Diet Green iguanas are mostly herbivores. Green leafy plants or ripe fruits are their preferred foods. They occasionally eat some carrion or invertebrates.

Fact Green iguanas are great swimmers. They use their tails to propel themselves in water. They can stay submerged for over 30 minutes.

Conservation status   Not evaluated

Common Chuckwalla

Sauromalus ater

Reptiles

Snakes and lizards

Lizards

Factfile

Habitat	Desert
Distribution	North America
Length	Up to 19 in
Clutch size	5 to 16 eggs
Life span	Up to 20 years
Predators	Coyotes, larger birds

Diet The chuckwalla's diet is mostly made up of plant matter. They enjoy flowers, buds, leaves and fruit. They will infrequently consume a few insects.

Fact When disturbed, a chuckwalla will gulp air and wedge itself into a rock crevice. It inflates its body with air in order to protect itself.

Conservation status   **Least concern**

Reptiles

Snakes and lizards

Lizards

Viviparous Lizard

Zootoca vivipara

Factfile

Habitat	Desert, savannah, marsh, rivers, lakes
Distribution	Europe, northern Asia
Length	2 to 3 in
Litter size	3 to 10 live young
Life span	5 to 6 years
Predators	Snakes, hedgehogs, shrews, dogs, cats

Diet The viviparous lizard has a diet of invertebrates, mostly small insects. It shakes larger prey in its jaws before chewing it and swallowing whole.

Fact Females normally give birth in July. Their young are born in transparent membranes which split open during or immediately after birth.

Conservation status	**Not evaluated**

Texas Horned Lizard

Phrynosoma cornutum

Factfile

Habitat	Desert, grassland, prairies, scrubland
Distribution	North America
Length	3 to 6 in
Clutch size	Up to 40 eggs
Life span	8 to 12 years
Predators	Snakes, birds, foxes, dogs, coyotes

Diet The Texas horned lizard's diet is mostly made up of ants. They will supplement this diet with grasshoppers, isopods, beetles and beetle larvae.

Fact If threatened, this lizard will squirt blood from its eyes. The blood comes from ducts in the eyes and can travel a distance of up to 3 feet.

Conservation status	Least concern

104

Green Anole

Anolis carolinensis

Factfile

Habitat	Savannah, grassland, forest
Distribution	North America
Length	4 to 8 in
Clutch size	1 or 2 eggs
Life span	2 to 8 years
Predators	Birds, snakes, lizards, cats, dogs

Diet The green anole eats a variety of insects, including beetles and flies, as well as spiders and some arthropods. They also eat mollusks, grain and seeds.

Fact Male green anoles have pink dewlaps, folds of loose skin hanging from the neck, which they inflate in territorial displays and to attract a mate.

Conservation status   Least concern

Five-lined Skink

Plestiodon fasciatus

Factfile

Habitat	Forest
Distribution	USA
Length	5 to 8.5 in
Clutch size	15 to 18 eggs
Life span	Up to 6 years
Predators	Birds, snakes, raccoons, foxes, skunks, cats

Diet Five-lined skinks mostly eat insects such as crickets, grasshoppers and beetles. They also feed on snails, frogs, lizards and newborn mice.

Fact Skinks hibernate alone or in small groups during the winter months. They do this in hiding holes in decaying logs, under rocks or underground.

Conservation status   Least concern

Broad-headed Skink

Plestiodon laticeps

Factfile

Habitat	Forest
Distribution	USA
Length	Up to 13 in
Clutch size	8 to 22 eggs
Life span	Up to 8 years
Predators	Birds, cats, larger reptiles

Diet Broad-headed skinks eat many different insects, arachnids, mollusks, rodents and smaller reptiles. They even eat the young of their own species.

Fact Broad-headed skinks are arboreal, spending their lives in trees. They only occasionally come down to the ground to forage for food.

Conservation status   **Not evaluated**

Eastern Blue-tongued Skink

Tiliqua scincoides

Factfile

Habitat	Grassland, forest, rain forest, desert
Distribution	Australia
Length	12 to 24 in
Litter size	6 to 20 live young
Life span	Up to 20 years
Predators	Birds, snakes, cats, dogs

Diet The eastern blue-tongue's diet includes vegetation, berries, flowers and insects. They also eat snails by crushing the shell and swallowing the soft body.

Fact When threatened, this skink puffs up its body, sticks out its blue tongue and hisses. It may also flatten out its body to appear too large to attack.

Conservation status   **Not evaluated**

Stump-tailed Skink

Tiliqua rugosa

Habitat	Plains, woodland
Distribution	Australia
Length	14 to 18 in
Litter size	1 to 3 live young
Life span	10 to 14 years
Predators	Cats, dogs

Diet The stump-tailed skink has a varied diet of plant matter, such as herbs and seedlings, insects and other arthropods, snails and some carrion.

Fact Stump-tailed skinks often have to face droughts and famines. The tail acts as a fat store to help the lizard survive in times when food is scarce.

Conservation status   **Not evaluated**

Giant Ameiva

Ameiva ameiva

Factfile

Habitat	Savannah, grassland, rain forest
Distribution	Central and South America
Length	18 to 20 in
Clutch size	3 to 6 eggs
Life span	3 to 5 years
Predators	Birds, snakes, mongooses, cats

Diet Giant ameivas are active foragers. Animals found in their diet include beetles, larvae, grasshoppers, spiders, butterflies and termites.

Fact They mainly avoid predators by running away. They are very fast and can run on their hind legs. At night they retreat to burrows for safety.

Conservation status   **Not evaluated**

Six-lined Racerunner

Cnemidophorus sexlineatus

Factfile

Habitat	Savannah, grassland, desert
Distribution	USA
Length	Up to 12 in
Clutch size	1 to 6 eggs
Life span	Up to 6 years
Predators	Snakes, birds, small mammals

Diet The six-lined racerunner has a diet containing insects, arthropods and snails. It feeds on many grasshoppers, flies, crickets and moths.

Fact Six-lined racerunners are very fast. They can reach speeds of up to 12 miles per hour. They use their speed to run away from any danger.

Conservation status — **Least concern**

Komodo Dragon
Varanus komodoensis

Reptiles

Snakes and lizards

Lizards

Factfile

Habitat	Savannah, grassland, forest
Distribution	Indonesian archipelago
Length	Up to 10 ft
Clutch size	Up to 20 eggs
Life span	Up to 50 years
Predators	No natural predators

Diet An adult komodo dragon eats a variety of large prey, including goats, pigs, deer, horses, water buffalo and smaller komodo dragons.

Fact The komodo dragon produces poisonous venom similar to that of a snake. Once bitten, the prey cannot escape far as the venom acts quickly.

Conservation status   **Vulnerable**

Nile Monitor

Varanus niloticus

Factfile

Habitat	Woodland, savannah, scrubland, swamp
Distribution	Sub-Saharan Africa
Length	Up to 8 ft
Clutch size	Up to 60 eggs
Life span	10 to 20 years
Predators	Crocodiles, pythons

Diet Nile monitors will eat frogs, toads, rodents, fish, lizards, small turtles, birds and their eggs, beetles, crabs and some slugs. They also steal crocodile eggs.

Fact Female Nile monitors will dig holes in termite mounds and lay a clutch of eggs inside. The heat from the termites acts to incubate the eggs.

Conservation status   **Not evaluated**

Lace l lonitor

Varanus varius

Reptiles

Snakes and lizards

Lizards

Factfile

Habitat   Forests, coast
Distribution Eastern Australia
Length   5 to 6.5 ft
Clutch size   4 to 14 eggs
Life span   Up to 14 years
Predators   Snakes, dingoes

Diet The lace monitor has a broad and varied diet including birds, insects, bird eggs, reptiles and small mammals. They will also eat carrion, including road kill.

Fact Lace monitors have toes with long, strong claws, which are used for climbing. Monitors are the only lizards that have a forked tongue like a snake.

Conservation status   **Least concern**

Water Monitor
Varanus salvator

Factfile

Habitat   Rivers, streams
Distribution   Southern Asia
Length   5 to 10 ft
Clutch size   Up to 20 eggs
Life span   Up to 10 years
Predators   Crocodiles, large snakes, otters

Diet Water monitors eat birds and their eggs, small mammals (especially rats), fish, lizards, frogs, snakes, juvenile crocodiles and tortoises.

Fact While hunting for aquatic prey, the water monitor can remain submerged for up to 30 minutes without coming to the surface to take in air.

Conservation status   **Least concern**

White-throated Monitor

Varanus albigularis

Reptiles

Snakes and lizards

Lizards

Factfile

Habitat	Savannah, woodland, open forest
Distribution	Africa
Length	Up to 6.5 ft
Clutch size	Up to 50 eggs
Life span	Up to 20 years
Predators	Large snakes, birds

Diet White-throated monitors hunt for small reptiles and mammals, bird eggs and insects. They will also eat carrion if they come across it.

Fact White-throated monitors rub their chins on millipedes before eating them. They do this to remove the foul fluid that the millipede excretes.

Conservation status   **Least concern**

Chinese Crocodile Lizard

Shinisaurus crocodilurus

Factfile

Habitat	Shallow pools in forests
Distribution	China, Vietnam
Length	Up to 1.5 ft
Litter size	2 to 6 live young
Life span	Up to 10 years
Predators	Birds, mammals

Diet
The Chinese crocodile lizard hunts in shallow water or in vegetation. It survives on a diet of various insects, snails, tadpoles and some worms.

Fact
The Chinese crocodile lizard is named for the appearance of its tail. It has a large pair of scales running in ridges down its length like a crocodile.

Conservation status	Not evaluated

American Alligator

Alligator mississippiensis

Factfile

Habitat	Lakes, swamp, marsh
Distribution	Southeastern USA
Length	10 to 15 ft
Clutch size	35 to 88 eggs
Life span	35 to 50 years
Predators	Snakes, birds, raccoons (young only)

Diet Adult American alligators consume fish, turtles, snakes, and small mammals. The young tend to have a diet of insects, snails and small fish.

Fact American alligators hunt in the water at night. They swallow small prey whole. Large prey are dragged underwater, drowned and then eaten in pieces.

Conservation status   **Least concern**

118

Chinese Alligator

Alligator sinensis

Factfile

Habitat	Lakes, ponds, rivers, streams
Distribution	Central Pacific coast of China
Length	4.5 to 7 ft
Clutch size	10 to 40 eggs
Life span	Up to 50 years
Predators	Alligators, fish, birds (young only)

Diet Adult Chinese alligators prey on fish, snails, clams, small mammals and waterfowl. Younger alligators eat insects and other small invertebrates.

Fact The Chinese alligator is one of the smallest and one of the most endangered crocodilians. There are more of them in zoos than in the wild.

Conservation status **Critically endangered**

Dwarf Crocodile

Osteolaemus tetraspis

Reptiles

Crocodilians

Crocodiles

Factfile

Habitat	Ponds, swamp
Distribution	West Africa
Length	Up to 5.5 ft
Clutch size	Up to 20 eggs
Life span	50 to 100 years
Predators	Mongooses, larger crocodiles

Diet Dwarf crocodiles enjoy a varied diet. Fish, birds, frogs, toads and crustaceans make up the bulk of their food, as well as the occasional mammal.

Fact Dwarf crocodiles are as happy living in the water as they are on land. These small crocodiles can hold their breath for up to half an hour underwater.

Conservation status **Vulnerable**

Nile Crocodile
Crocodylus niloticus

Factfile

Habitat	Rivers, freshwater marsh, mangrove swamp
Distribution	Saharan Africa, the Nile Basin, Madagascar
Length	Up to 20 ft
Clutch size	25 to 80 eggs
Life span	Up to 45 years
Predators	No natural predators

Diet The diet of the Nile crocodile is mainly fish, but it will attack almost anything that crosses its path, such as zebras, small hippos, porcupines and birds.

Fact A sleeping crocodile often cools off by keeping its mouth open. Birds often gather around and pick off insects and meat from its teeth.

Conservation status　　　　**Least concern**

Saltwater Crocodile
Crocodylus porosus

Reptiles

Crocodilians

Crocodiles

Factfile

Habitat	Coastal water, rivers, billabongs, swamp
Distribution	Australia, Southeast Asia, India
Length	Up to 23 ft
Clutch size	40 to 60 eggs
Life span	Up to 70 years
Predators	Humans

Diet This crocodile's diet includes crustaceans, turtles, lizards, snakes and birds. The young eat insects, amphibians, fish, crustaceans and reptiles.

Fact A sedated saltwater crocodile in a Taiwanese zoo bit a veterinarian's forearm off. After hours of surgery, it was successfully reattached.

Conservation status   **Least concern**

Black Caiman
Melanosuchus niger

Factfile

Habitat	Rivers, lakes, swamps
Distribution	North and central South America
Length	Up to 20 ft
Clutch size	Up to 40 eggs
Life span	30 to 40 years
Predators	Jaguars

Diet Fish, such as piranhas and catfish, make up a large part of the adult black caiman's diet. Young individuals tend to feed on insects and crustaceans.

Fact The black caiman is unique among crocodilians as the color it has when young – yellowish stripes and spots – is retained into its adult life.

Conservation status   **Least concern**

Spectacled Caiman

Caiman crocodilus

Factfile

Habitat	Most freshwater habitats
Distribution	Central and South America
Length	5 to 7 ft
Clutch size	10 to 40 eggs
Life span	30 to 40 years
Predators	Jaguars

Diet Spectacled caimans have a varied diet. Their prey includes insects, snails, shrimp, crabs, fish, lizards, snakes, turtles, birds and small mammals.

Fact The spectacled caiman derives its name from the bony ridge that runs between its eyes. This ridge resembles a pair of spectacles.

Conservation status   **Least concern**

Gharial
Gavialis gangeticus

Factfile

Habitat	Slow-moving backwaters of rivers
Distribution	Northern Indian subcontinent
Length	12.5 to 16 ft
Clutch size	20 to 100 eggs
Life span	40 to 60 years
Predators	Humans

Diet The gharial's diet is made up mainly of fish. They supplement their diet by hunting for the occasional insect and some small animals.

Fact Gharials spend most of their time in water as they have short legs that make it difficult to raise their bodies off the ground in order to walk far.

Conservation status   **Endangered**

Glossary

Amphibians Vertebrates that live both on land and in water.

Arachnids A group of arthropods with eight legs. Examples include spiders, scorpions, mites and ticks.

Arboreal To live in trees.

Arthropods A group of invertebrates with segmented bodies, external skeletons and jointed limbs. Examples include insects, spiders and crustaceans.

Billabong A stagnant pool of water in the bed of a stream that does not flow steadily.

Birds of prey Carnivorous birds that hunt and kill other animals.

Bivalves Animals that have two hinged shells. Examples include clams, mussels, oysters and scallops.

Camouflage Colors or patterns that allow an animal to blend in with its background.

Carapace A hard shield on the back of an animal's body.

Carnivorous To feed on the flesh of other animals.

Carrion The remains of dead animals.

Clutch A nest of eggs.

Constrictors Snakes that kill by coiling around their prey and squeezing until it cannot breathe.

Crustaceans Arthropods such as lobsters or crabs with jointed legs and two pairs of antennae.

Exoskeletons An external skeleton that supports and protects an animal's body.

Habitat The natural home of a species.

Herbivorous To eat only plants.

Hibernate To spend the winter in a sleeplike state.

Incubate The maintaining of a constant temperature during the development of the embryo.

Insectivores Carnivores that eat insects.

Invertebrates Animals without backbones.

Isopods A group of crustaceans characterized by a flattened body with seven pairs of legs.

Keystone species A species of animal on which other species in an ecosystem depend.

Marsupials Mammals such as kangaroos and wombats, who give birth to tiny, underdeveloped young that grow inside a pouch.

Metabolism The chemical processes that occur within animals in order to maintain life.

Migration To move from one habitat to another.

Mollusk A soft-bodied invertebrate such as a snail, often with a hard shell.

Molt The shedding of skin to allow growth.

Musk A greasy secretion produced by some animals, with a powerful odor.

Nocturnal Active at night.

Omnivore An animal that feeds on plant and animal matter.

Ovoviviparous A way of reproduction in animals where embryos develop inside eggs that are retained within the mother's body until they are ready to hatch.

Predators Animals that kill and eat other animals.

Prey An animal hunted by predators.

Regenerate The process of restoring and growing that recreates damaged tissues or organs.

Salps Tiny, floating marine animals with transparent bodies with an opening at each end.

Savannah Hot grassland in Africa.

Scavenge To find and collect items of food.

Semiaquatic To survive equally well in water or on land.

Spurs Stiff, usually sharp, horny appendages on the leg of an animal.

Toxic A poisonous substance.

Venom Poison injected from one animal into another through fangs or a sting.

Vertebrates Animals with a backbone or spinal column. Examples include fish, amphibians, reptiles, birds and mammals.

Viviparous Producing living young instead of eggs from within the body in the manner of nearly all mammals, many reptiles and a few fish.

Index